RESTAURANT OPERATIONS
Made Easy

Step-by-step guide on how to run a restaurant business

KUFRE BASSEY

Restaurant Operations Made Easy

ISBN-13: 9798333440334

Published by: Peace Book Publishing

Printed in the United States of America

Dedication

This book is dedicated first to my late parents for giving me the opportunity to be educated .

I also dedicate the book to aspiring restaurant managers and those that want to own a restaurant business.

Acknowledgements

First, I want to thank God Almighty for giving me the grace and inspiration to write this book.

Next, I want to appreciate my lovely wife, Joyce Bassey, for her encouragement and support. I love you, my queen.

I would like to express my deepest gratitude to my late parents, Mr and Mrs Daniel Bassey, for their unwavering support, prayers, and encouragement during their time with me.

I also want to thank my spiritual parents, Pastor and Mrs Uzo Enelamah of RCCG House of Praise Lekki, for always encouraging their spiritual children to become authors. I pray for more grace and anointing for you.

A very special thanks to my operation managers: Mr Blessing Bassey, Mr Bolaji Olatunji, and Mr Ayodele Oluwole for reviewing the manuscript. To Mr Wale Mutiu and Mrs Adefunke Adebisi, my area coaches, I say a big thank you for taking out time to review the manuscript too.

I also would like to thank my restaurant business coach, Mr Abhishek Kumar, for writing the foreword.

God bless you, sir.

A special appreciation goes to my late aunt, Mrs Comfort Bassey, and my late uncle, Mr Sunday Bassey. To my siblings, cousins, niece, and nephew; thank you for your support and prayers. God bless you all my family.

Lastly, this book would not be complete if I fail to thank my editor, Mrs Peace Isaac- Udofia, and Eno Sam, founder of BEWA Africa. Your encouragement and coaching made this book become a reality. God bless you.

Foreword

Wow! This is a detailed comprehensive know-how for individuals who wish to learn how the restaurant industry works and operates.

Kufre Bassey is one of the restaurant professionals with strong business acumen.

Thanks, Kufre, for disclosing the basic details of running a successful restaurant.

Wishing you the very best! Abhishek Kumar

Seasoned QSR professional

Table of Contents

INTRODUCTION

'The business of feeding people is the most amazing business in the world.'
—*José Andrés*

Figure 1: An empty menu board

Over the years, many restaurant managers and owners have found it difficult to run their restaurants effectively. Owning a restaurant is not all about serving hot and delicious meals. It's not about serving crispy chicken, baking cakes that melt in the mouth, moulding swallows attractively, or serving mouthwatering fisherman soup. Neither is it all about offering amazing discounts and satisfying customers. It's also not limited to having your staff dress in uniform and smiling at every customer that walks in. It's a lot more.

Like any other business, a restaurant is meant to generate sales and profits for the owner. If there is no profit, it would go out of business. To stay in business, there are certain things you must *know* and *do*.

Are you a restaurant owner? Do you want to learn the ropes of running a restaurant effectively? Whether it's a food truck business, a small snack bar, or a large eatery you own or manage, this book will enlighten and guide you on how to run a smooth food business.

'Restaurant Operations Made Easy' stems from my years of experience as a restaurant manager. So far, I can tell you managing a restaurant is not a walk in the park but with the right knowledge and tools, you can get it right from the word go. And that's why I wrote this book – to equip you with the right knowledge and tools to take your restaurant to the next level.

CHAPTER 1

RESTAURANT OPERATIONS

Restaurant operations can be defined as the day-to-day activities that occur in a restaurant. These activities include purchasing, preparation, service, accounting, and cleaning. The way these activities are carried out will determine if a restaurant will make sales or not.

Imagine a restaurant with dirty plates on tables, chicken and fish bones on the floor, dusty counters, grumpy-looking staff members speaking harshly to customers, and serving meals with spoiled fish and other expired condiments. You'll surely run out of business because no one wants to visit a dirty restaurant with grumpy staff that serves spoiled food!

I like to see restaurant operations as a football match where the coach (the restaurant owner or manager) determines the team or player formation to use to win the match of the day. If the staff in a restaurant are not well-positioned in its various departments, the restaurant will not make sales.

This shows that to have a restaurant running smoothly via restaurant operations, we need the right teammates – staff.

HIRING THE RIGHT TEAM

"I can tell in two minutes if I should hire someone in the kitchen. Two minutes. It's his desire. It's that open-eyed, attentive expression. If he doesn't have it … I mean, I can teach a chimp how to cook dinner. But I cannot teach a chimp how to love it."

— ***Mario Batal***

Figure 2: Bartenders

Hiring the right team for your restaurant business is

vital because one bad hired staff (cook, cleaner, driver, cashier, etc) can ruin the business. My advice to restaurant owners and managers has always been for them to scrutinize applicants before employment. Staff members of a restaurant are key tools needed to run a successful restaurant operation.

I need to sound a note of warning here. Never employ workers when you are desperately in need of them because you'll hire the wrong one. Through my years of experience as a restaurant manager, I have learned to employ enough manpower in the business. Due to the nature of the business, you will always have a high staff turnover. Some people see restaurant jobs as an opportunity to raise funds for projects e.g school fees. They have it in mind to work for at least six months after which they resign. Also, work hours discourage people from working long term. Working in the restaurant barely gives you enough time for family, your dreams, and rest. Holidays are sales peak times for restaurants and over time, some workers may feel the need to create more time for family and to pursue their dreams.

Hence, it is always advisable you have backup staff,

the same way football coaches have reserve players on the bench.

There are certain things to watch out for when hiring. Amongst other things, experience, competency, and attitude towards work are crucial. You can tell if an applicant is the right one for the job through his/her body language when you dish out job tasks and the difficult part of the job. Also, if an applicant asks about salary early on in the interview, see it as a red flag.

A young lady applied for the position of customer service attendant in a restaurant some years back. It's customary for interviewers to ask for salary expectations during interviews. This lady jumped the gun and asked the interviewer how much her salary would be. Anyway, she was employed because of her knowledge and experience. Along the line, she became irritable and eventually flared up one day when given a task. Complaining bitterly about the job, she said she was tired of the job. She said she only accepted it because of the money. That day, her employer regretted employing her.

Companies need passionate employees willing to

add value. Never hire out of pity or sentiments! Hire right and you will get the best of employees in return.

CHAPTER 2

TOOLS NEEDED FOR OPERATION

"It's not the load that breaks you down, it's the way you carry it."
— ***Lou Holtz***

Figure 3: A Checklist

For seamless restaurant operations, you need certain tools. Imagine a student in maths class without a pen and a notebook to solve problems with. There is no way the student will enjoy the class. He might have to run around asking for an extra pen and notebook because they are vital for gaining in the class. In the same vein, a manager, supervisor, or restaurateur needs the right tools for smooth restaurant operations.

Six tools are needed daily for smooth restaurant operations. The tools are:

1. Operations Manual
2. Checklist
3. Pocket jotter
4. Staff roster
5. Production projection
6. Thermometer

1. Operations Manual

This is a manual that contains every activity to be carried out daily at different intervals. It acts as a guide for managers, supervisors, or restaurateurs, making them know what they ought to do daily. The operations manual should be worked on every hour because there is a tendency for you to encounter one issue or the other. Every issue encountered must be fixed immediately. Also, it's important to follow the operations manual to the letter. This will enable you to tackle problems in the restaurant before auditors show up (more on this later).

2. Checklist

This is a printed list of tasks a worker is supposed to carry out daily. It is also similar to the operations manual. A newly employed worker can easily work with the aid of a checklist without much supervision.

3. Pocket Jotter

This is a small jotter used as a to-do list by a manager or supervisor. It helps you work smart and manage time. It also makes you more efficient and organized.

4. Staff Roster

This is a crucial tool in the restaurant business. A staff roster enables your staff to know their schedule and the shift they would run each day. It also tells when each member of staff will observe his/her off duty.

The staff roster is like the game of chess. Like chess pieces, staff must be positioned strategically to win the game for the day. As you wouldn't move chess pieces randomly on the board, you wouldn't randomly fix the staff roster. If the staff are not well scheduled and positioned in the various departments, it will affect the sales of that day.

Also, workers have different strengths. In the game of chess, we have the queen, knight, rook, king, bishop, and pawn with the queen as the most powerful piece. The queen is the strongest attacking piece, she can move any number of squares in any direction and she is worth nine points which equals nine pawns. Losing her would be a disaster! In the same vein, there are staff members that are more experienced, creative, can solve problems and make decisions quickly, etc. Positioning them rightly will give your business a boom because they partner with you to make your business flourish. Losing them may not be good for your business. This shouldn't be an excuse to push the other team members behind. They must be encouraged to grow.

5. Production Projection

This is a projection system that enables the production staff to know the quantity of food to produce at a particular time. You can know this through the products sold the previous day. With this knowledge, you'll know how much should be produced on that day. This enables you to minimise wastage and increase profit for your business.

6. Thermometer

This is also a tool that is important in carrying out successful restaurant operations. With the help of a thermometer, you can determine if your walk-in chiller or your cold room is attaining the right temperature which is -18°C to -23°C and 2°C to 4°C respectively. You can also use a thermometer to test the temperature of your hot cabinet warmer.

There are several other tools you can use in restaurant operations but the six mentioned above can help you run successful restaurant operations without stress.

CHAPTER 3

AREAS OF OPERATIONS

"A well-run restaurant is like a winning baseball team. It makes the most of every crew member's talent and takes advantage of every split-second opportunity to speed up service."
— ***David Ogilvy***

In chapter one, I likened restaurant operations to a football field where the coach determines the team or player formation to use to win the match of the day. As a coach, he determines who plays as a striker (in front) and who plays as a defender (behind). The restaurant business is structured the same way.

The restaurant is divided into two key areas, which are the front of house area and the back of house area. They are also known as FOH and BOH in the short form respectively.

FRONT OF HOUSE AREA

Figure 4: Food counter

The front-of-house area is an area that shows the image of the restaurant. The front-of-house area comprises the car pack area, customer restroom, the lobby section, and the cash point section (a.k.a the food counter area).

These areas are very important because they reveal to the customers how the restaurant is and it also determines if they will patronize your restaurant or not. The customer service attendant and the lobby host must be smartly dressed, clean, and cheerful because they are the first set of workers the customers will meet. Remember the saying, 'first impression matters'? The same applies here. The front of house staff must be well represented.

The front of house area must be clean with a pleasant ambience to enable customers to be comfortable dining in your restaurant and have a reason to return. The percentage of staff needed at the front of house is **60**% to ensure all customers are served on time. How you manage your FOH can determine if your restaurant will be successful in the long run.

BACK OF HOUSE AREA

Figure 5: Kitchen sections

The back of house which is also known as BOH is the powerhouse of the restaurant where production and other activities that are out of the sight of customers take place. The back of house area comprises the kitchen, the dishwashing section, the manager's office, staff cloakroom, security office, dry store, generator area, and water plant area.

The kitchen sections and the dry store are the most important because they are the powerhouse of the restaurant. The kitchen sections must be spacious with well-aligned equipment to allow easy movement because it's usually busy, especially on weekends (This depends on your environment).

The staff in the kitchen department must be well trained and positioned rightly. Badly cooked meals prepared from the kitchen and taken out to the counter (the front of house) can disrupt the business for the day. Therefore, there is a need for all kitchen staff to be careful when preparing meals.

The percentage of staff needed at the back of the house is **40**% to ensure all meals are well prepared and served on time. This percentage also helps you assign tasks easily. You must encourage communication between the FOH staff and BOH staff as their jobs are different. Poor communication between them can upset customers and eventually affect sales for the day.

CHAPTER 4

WALK OF 8

"As a restaurateur, my job is to basically control the chaos and the drama. There's always going to be chaos in the restaurant business."
— ***Rocco DiSpirito***

Walk of 8 is an operational walk that has to do with the work and activities of the day. As an operation manager, I learnt this long ago from my superiors (i.e restaurant general manager, area coach, and regional manager) in the various restaurants I have worked in. For restaurant operations to be successful, you must take a walk of 8 which begins as soon as you step into the restaurant premises either from the front of house or from the back of house.

Now, let's assume you get into the restaurant via the front of house (FOH). The first area to check is your car park lot. It must be clean and free of illegal occupants that can pose a threat to your customers when they drive in or out. Illegal occupants could be hawkers, touts, etc.

Next, you check the lobby – where guests/customers sit to eat – for cleanliness and a pleasant ambience. Afterwards, walk into the customers' restrooms and ensure they've been cleaned by the lobby host/hostess using their pasted checklist. Lastly, check the food counter section to ensure all the food products are available and also check the cash point area for the cashier's readiness (outward appearance and demeanor) to serve customers. These last two areas must be clean too.

Still on the Walk of 8, move to the back of the house (BOH). First, check the kitchen for cleanliness. Then check the food produced to ensure the production staff adheres to the recipe and follows the standard way of doing things in the restaurant. Thereafter, move to the cold room or walk-in-chiller and check if the cold room is at the right temperature using the thermometer. Also, check the perishables to confirm they are fresh. Next, move to check the generator and the dustbin area. The dustbin area must be free of flies, overflowing/ scattered garbage, and offensive odour. Lastly, walk into the dry store and check for expired products or critical items in the store that needs to be ordered. Also, ensure the items in the store are well arranged. The above exercise can also start from the back of the house and end at the front of the house, using your operations manual as a guide. When you carry out the walk of 8 daily, you can be sure of running a successful restaurant business with less stress.

CHAPTER 5

STAFF TRAINING

"The only thing worse than training your employees and having them leave is not training them and having them stay"
–Henry Ford, Founder of Ford Motor Company

Figure 6: Staff training

According to the Cambridge dictionary, training is the process of learning the skills you need to do a particular job or activity.

The importance of training in the restaurant business or any other profession can not be over-emphasized. Training is key for a successful business. Everyone needs training on the job – managers, supervisors, all workers as well as the restaurant owner.

IMPORTANCE OF TRAINING

1. Increases efficiency

2. Increases staff morale

3. Increases profitability

4. Reduces staff turnover

5. Develops talents

1. Increases efficiency

Trained staff become confident in their work. This in the long run increases productivity.

2. Reduces loss

Food loss is a huge problem in the restaurant business. Food loss is wasted food which equals a waste of money. Training staff on monitoring refrigerator and hot cabinet warmer temperatures; implementing a 'First-in first-out (FIFO) system, etc, can reduce food loss greatly.

N.B FIFO means food stored the longest gets used first.

3. Increases profitability

Training helps staff know how to treat customers better. Well-treated customers become repeat customers which means more money for the business. Also, great customer service results in positive reviews on your social media handles.

4. Reduces Staff turnover

Training makes staff feel important. Employees trained continuously end up happier. This shows off in their work.

5. Develops Talents

Teaching your staff new skills may cause potential talents to spring forth.

Cleaner exhibiting leadership quality has the potential to become a manager in the future.

A waiter with a culinary interest has the potential of

becoming a master chef in the future. Nurturing these talents will do your restaurant good.

When a worker is first employed in a restaurant, he/she undergoes an IQ test to ascertain their level of reasoning and writing ability. This is also referred to as employee onboarding. This exercise makes you know as a manager or restaurant owner the area he/she will need help. Also, a newly employed worker in the restaurant must receive induction training and on-the-job training.

Induction training: This is the first training a newly employed worker undergoes before commencing work in the restaurant. Induction is also a way of introducing the new employee to the company. In this training, facilitators give the employee basic orientation about the company and the job. After the training, the facilitators give the employee tests on what was taught to measure his/her comprehension.

On-the-job training: This training has to do with the primary assignment of the staff.

To ensure a newly employed worker learns properly, he/she is attached to an experienced worker. This is called buddy training. The buddy trainer guides the newbie through his responsibility and answers any questions he asks.

As a manager or restaurateur, you must train your staff internally and externally to enable them to deliver well and add value to the organization. This book is a result of the various training sessions I've had as a manager over the years. Yes, training isn't a walk in the park. It is time-consuming and costs money but it pays.

You can also train your staff by creating a session I call 'build know-how'.

Build know-how is about exposing your staff to many things on the job and throwing questions to ensure they understand what was taught. Investing your time and resources in the training of your staff will not only add value to them or your company but will attract more customers to your restaurant.

When is the right time to train your staff and build know-how? You can train and build know-how early in the morning and during non peak periods (periods when you have shorter customer queues). Also, you need to devote some minutes every morning for some pet talk with your staff members. This allows you the opportunity to discuss what went well or wrong in the previous day's work and your expectations for the day. Pet talk is also another way of training your staff.

There are two key areas your staff needs training:

1. Customer service
2. Product quality

Customer service

Every staff member (whether FOH or BOH) in the restaurant needs customer service training. Your customer service attendant, also known as cashier, needs the training more because they are the first contact with the customer. Their service influences customers a great deal.

Product quality training

This training is meant for the kitchen staff because they render customer service with their products. Customers will keep coming to your restaurant as long as the food is tasteful. You will never know staff can do something well until you train them.

Other kinds of training include soft skills, technology, and safety training.

CHAPTER 6

FORECASTING AND PROJECTION

Planning is bringing the future into the present so that you can do something about it now."
— **Alan Lakein, author**

Figure 7: Planning ahead

Forecasting and projection are ways of knowing your sales figures for the day and the quantity of food you want to produce. It enables you to achieve the sales figures for that day.

Forecasting and projection can also be used to know

your daily, monthly, and yearly sales target. It is like setting a SMART goal for yourself daily, monthly, and yearly. The goal must be Specific, Measurable, Achievable, Relevant, and Time-bound. It is important your forecasting and Projection are accurate.

Now, what are forecasting and projection?

FORECASTING

This is a weekly or monthly sales prediction you conduct for your restaurant using a day's sales to calculate the same days and average for four weeks, following the sales trend of your restaurant. For example, the sales figure the restaurant makes on Wednesday will be used to calculate other Wednesday sales in the previous week. Then you divide it by the four weeks in a month to get the forecasted sales for each day.

In other words, you add four days back sales in four weeks generated from your POS system and divide them by the four weeks to get your average sales for each day. That will be your sales forecast for the new month.

Below are four factors to consider when preparing

your forecast:

1. Level of manpower
2. Availability of raw materials
3. Public holidays/ community events
4. Unusual weather

1. Level of manpower

For you to achieve an accurate forecast for the month, you will need to have the right number of staff available. They must be well positioned in the right sections according to their level of experience on the job. Without the right number of staff on ground, the sales target will be affected and you'll also end up with dissatisfied customers.

2. Availability of raw material

When placing an order for raw materials, you need to know the quantity of each stock you need – week or month – that will enable you to achieve your sales target for the month (More on this in the next chapter).

3. Public holidays/community events

As far as the restaurant business is concerned, public holidays must be well utilized when preparing your forecast. It also determines if your staff will produce more on that day or less to avoid waste and loss of sales.

4. Unusual weather

This must also be put into consideration when preparing your forecast (especially during the rainy seasons).

PROJECTION

This is similar to forecasting because it is also a way of predicting the number of products to produce at a given time using the forecasted sales for the day. To achieve an accurate projection, you will need a previous day's, week's, and month's record of sold products to determine the projection for the day.

The same factors to be considered when forecasting above also affects your projections if not properly put into consideration. Projections that are not properly planned can lead to loss of sales or wastage.

The major difference between forecasting and projections is that forecasting is used for sales prediction while projection is used for product prediction.

CHAPTER 7

ORDERING SYSTEM

"You don't have to cook fancy or complicated masterpieces - just good food from fresh ingredients."
— **Julia Child**

Figure 8: A local market

The ordering system is the method you use as a manager or a restaurateur in ordering raw materials from the local market or international market. The ordering system in a restaurant is important because it determines the availability of raw materials in the store and what will be on the menu for the day.

Before you think of ordering your raw materials and packages, you need to have a purchasing and a store/logistics manager to carry out the ordering effectively. You also need to decide whether to order your raw materials through a supplier or purchase them bit by bit from the nearby market. I strongly advise you to deal with a supplier directly and also buy in bulk because you will get a reasonable profit at the end of the day.

There are four key things to consider before ordering your raw materials and packages. They are:

1. The space in your store

2. Your daily, weekly, and monthly usage

3. Use by date of every product

4. Internal transfer (if any).

1. The space in your store

This is the first thing you need to put into consideration when placing an order for any product. Your storage space could be the dry store, walk-in freezer, or walk-in chiller. The storage level (according to the standard for storing in any of the afore-mentioned storage) must be six inches from the floor and two inches away from the wall because no item should be kept on the floor to avoid cross-contamination.

2. Daily, weekly and monthly usage

This will give you an idea of the quantity of raw materials or packages to buy. You can find this out by checking the quantity of every product sold per day, week and month through the menu mix on your POS system. It is also important that you include 10% buffer stock after knowing what you use on a daily, weekly, and monthly basis. Buffer stock is an operational emergency stock you add to whatever you are ordering for the day, week, and month. It is important in case of bulk orders or an influx of customers. Knowing your stock usage will enable you to order right and also make good sales and reduce wastage.

3. Use by date

 The use by date reveals when a product is no more safe for consumption. It is the last date a product is approved for use. Purchasing items with use by dates close to the time of purchase will lead to food loss. Knowledge of use by date prevents loss of products and funds.

4. **Internal transfer** (if any)

This is the process of transferring out any item in the store to a sister company (in case your restaurant has another outlet). It must be documented in a transfer-out booklet (More on this in the next chapter).

To make good sales and to avoid running out of raw materials in your restaurant, you must get the ordering system right.

CHAPTER 8

INVENTORY SYSTEM

"If you count all your assets you always show a profit."
—**Wilson Mizner**

Figure 9: A storekeeper

The inventory system in the restaurant business is an exercise that cannot be ruled out or taken for granted. It gives a clear picture of the goods you have at hand. In other words, an inventory system is about tracking your daily, weekly, and monthly stock.

Taking inventory starts from the first day the restaurant opens. You take inventory of equipment, cooking utensils, and raw materials used to start the business because, at the end of every month and each calendar year of your business, all must be accounted for. A restaurant that does not carry out inventory exercises should be ready for failure and close down of the restaurant. For your restaurant to be successful, you must take stock daily, weekly, and monthly. Inventory also allows you to know what has been used and what is left.

It is advisable to have your restaurant inventory both in soft copy and hard copy to secure data.

Inventory in a restaurant can be divided into two categories: product inventory and financial inventory.

Product inventory- This is the process whereby the store manager confirms each item supplied with the supplier. Then he receives them in the dry store. After which he arranges them on the stainless shelves in the dry store and labels them. All items in the store need to be well arranged according to their categories like raw materials on one side, packages on another side, cleaning materials and chemicals also on another side of the shelves. Do not keep anything on the floor.

This arrangement will help you (as a store manager or restaurant owner) have an accurate account of your stock. It will also help you know which item has reduced to enable you to place another order.

DOCUMENTS NEEDED FOR STOCK INVENTORY

The documents needed for stock inventory include:

1. Goods received note (GRN)
2. Stock receiving booklet
3. Store bin card
4. Store issuing voucher (SIV)
5. Transfer out booklet
6. Transfer in booklet.
7. Transfer to counter inventory.
8. Ordering docket.

1. Goods received note

This is a document you sign with the supplier at the point of receiving your goods. You should keep the original copy of this document and return the photocopy to the supplier for documentation and reconciliation purposes.

2. Stock receiving booklet

This is a booklet used in recording all incoming goods.

3. Store bin card

This is an inventory card used to capture goods received, goods issued out to sections in the restaurant, and goods transferred out to other outlets. The bin card must be opened and closed daily to know the balance stock at hand.

4. Store issuing voucher

This is a booklet used to issue out raw materials and packages to sections in the restaurant. It must be duly signed by the store manager and restaurant manager before the items can be released.

5. Transfer out booklet

This is a booklet used to record goods transferred

out to other outlets. It must be duly signed by the store manager and the restaurant manager.

6. Transfer in booklet

This is a booklet used to receive incoming goods from other outlets. It must be duly signed by the store manager.

The above documents are all inventory booklets that must be under the custody of the storekeeper for auditing and accountability purposes. The next documents are not under the custody of the store-keeper.

7. Transfer to counter booklet

Transfer to counter booklet is used to record products produced by kitchen staff and sent out to the counter for sale. It helps the customer service attendant track the number of products given to them.

This booklet is under the supervision of the restaurant supervisor and production supervisor (for big restaurants that differentiate their supervisors).

8. Ordering docket

This is just like the transfer to counter booklet but

this booklet does the opposite. An ordering docket is a small book in the form of a jotter that the customer service attendant uses to order food from the back of the house. This process helps maintain orderliness between the front of the house and back of the house staff and also for accountability purposes.

Financial inventory- Many restaurant owners and managers have lost funds due to improper handling of money. Financial inventory helps curb this loss. Financial inventory in a restaurant is the process of collecting cash from the cashiers and keeping it in the metal safe in the manager's office for the bank officials to pick up the following morning.

Three documents can be used to document how money is collected at the front of the house and how it is spent.

1. Cash composition form
2. Imprest analysis form
3. Financial template

1. Cash composition form

This is a well-designed document with a serial number on each page. It is used to perform cash pull or mop at the cashpoint area. In it, you record all banknotes and coin denominations collected from a cashier. This exercise is done at intervals to avoid theft among the cashiers and also external robbery when money is too much in the till.

When you carry out this process as a manager or supervisor, please note that the cashier you are performing the cash pull for must confirm the money first and sign before you do the same to avoid arguments later.

2. Imprest analysis form

This is a well-designed booklet with a serial number used to document every expense for the day. It must be duly signed by an authorized person. It is also important you have a soft copy of this document for data keeping and reconciliation purposes.

3. Financial template

This is a template used to record the sales figures made daily. It can be created both on hard copy and soft copy.

Using the documents listed above will ensure safe record keeping and proper handling of cash in your restaurant.

Other documents needed for inventory are:

4. Staff register

This is a register needed in the restaurant for all staff, including the managers and supervisors of the restaurant. In this register, staff record their time of resumption to work and the time of closing. One important reason why this needs to be in place in your restaurant is to enable you to know how many workers are in the work premises for that day for security reasons. It also enables you to have a track record of the staff that worked for a month. It also helps you prepare staff salaries at the end of the month.

5. Staff movement register

This is a register needed in case a staff member is sent to deliver a customer order outside the restaurant or any other errands by the management staff.

6. Diesel receiving record

This is also an important register needed in the restaurant. It keeps track of the diesel received at a time and enables you to monitor your diesel usage daily.

The above inventory documents must be used judiciously and effectively if you must carry out successful restaurant operations.

CHAPTER 9

STAFF RECOGNITION

"Your number one customers are your people. Look after employees first and then customers last."
— **Ian Hutchinson**

Figure 10: A bartender

Staff recognition means acknowledging and rewarding exceptional workers. It is a practice that should not be overlooked. It is said that when you learn to appreciate people in the little they do, it will encourage them and also give them the courage to do more.

I respect the Kentucky Fried Chicken (KFC) restaurant so much because they have made this practice part of their culture. One of their principles as a restaurant is to ' believe in all people' and this gives their staff a sense of belonging.

Restaurant jobs can be very tedious and stressful most especially during rush hours. It is therefore important you appreciate your workers and let them know you value them.

As a manager, I have learnt to always recognize my staff in the public and reprimand them in private. Doing this not only encourages your staff but it improves their morale and protects their self-esteem before their colleagues.

David Novak, in his book titled 'Taking People with You', talked about an experience that changed how he thought as a leader. Some years back, as the head of operations for Pepsi bottling, he had a roundtable meeting with a group of route salesmen in a plant in St. Louis over coffee and doughnuts. He asked a question about merchandising which is all about the displays and visibility gotten in convenience and grocery stores. Everyone in the room pointed to Bob as an expert in that area. Someone even testified that Bob had taught him a lot. Instead of beaming with pride, Bob had tears running down his face. It turned out that Bob had been working in the company for over forty years but he never knew anyone in the company felt that way about him. Sadly, at the time of the meeting, he was set to retire in two weeks! Always appreciate exceptional workers.

Recognition has brought me thus far in the industry. Some years ago, I started the restaurant job as a team member and I was recognized at different levels on the job. I was also promoted on the job from one position to another. Recognition has encouraged and given me strong willpower.

Recognizing your staff is important because it will help identify and retain the skilled workers in your company.

Recognition takes different forms:

1. Granting worker(s) special parking space in the restaurant premises.

2. Giving free lunch tickets

3. Gift packs

4. Salary raise

5. Promotion

As a restaurant manager or restauranteur, adopt recognition as a part of your culture and also make the restaurant fun for your staff to work comfortably. It's your responsibility as a leader to cast a leadership shadow in your restaurant by celebrating both small and big achievements in your restaurant.

Remember, an employee recognized for a job well done will want to do more and even go the extra mile on any task given to him/her.

CHAPTER 10

COMPLIANCE

"I think toilets are more important than temples. No matter how many temples we go to, we are not going to get salvation. We need to give priority to toilets and cleanliness."
— **Jairam Ramesh**

Figure 11: Cleaning the restaurant's kitchen

Compliance in the restaurant business is simply regulatory bodies or groups of people, well trained in the hospitality industry, inspecting restaurants to check if they are complying with the rules and standard way of operations in the food industry.

A restaurant that is not under any form of supervision and control from internal and external bodies can not function well because these bodies are like the eyes of the business.

The compliance team can be divided into two distinct groups and they are:

INTERNAL COMPLIANCE AND EXTERNAL COMPLIANCE

Internal compliance: This is a special team in a restaurant that is well trained for auditing the internal affairs of the restaurant. The major audit from the internal compliance is on the standard operating procedure(SOP). Under the standard operating procedure we have:

1. Food safety and hygiene
2. Customer service procedure
3. Environmental sanitation
4. Waste management and
5. Use of equipment

It is the core responsibility of the internal compliance team to ensure management staff and team are following the standard of the restaurant, using the above parameters. They also prepare the restaurant in a standard state before the external compliance team inspects. This is important because both bodies must be on the same page for the success of the restaurant. The internal compliance team also visits the restaurant every month to ensure they keep to the standard. They rate the restaurant on food safety and hygiene, customer service, cleanliness, water management, food storage, and ambience of the restaurant. This audit from the internal compliance team will actually determine if the restaurant is performing well or not.

External compliance: These are external regulators that inspect the performance of your restaurant once or twice a year. They are also known as restaurant watchdogs, as they ensure all restaurants in the city comply with the rules and regulations guiding the food industry. In this book, I will identify three major bodies and regulators (in Nigeria) that you will often see in your restaurant. They are NAFDAC, REFSPAN and LASEPA.

NAFDAC: The National Agency for Food and Drug Administration and Control is a strong compliance team that ensures restaurants and other food companies are not serving expired food products to the public and are maintaining food safety and hygiene practices.

REFSPAN: Restaurant and Food Services Proprietors Association of Nigeria, previously known as AFFCON, is a non-profit and non-government organization that was set up in Nigeria to ensure that restaurants comply with the rules and regulations that govern the restaurant business. They also inspect the standard and operation of restaurants. Your restaurant must be a registered member of this body to enable you to operate well in the city as a restaurant owner.

LASEPA: It is the responsibility of The Lagos State Environmental Protection Agency to build sound environmental project in the development of sustainable environment. Their core responsibility is to ensure proper environmental sanitation in food premises. When they come to your restaurant and notice that the environment is not as clean as they expect it to be, they will seal your restaurant. You'd have to pay a fine for going against the standard before they can reopen your restaurant.

COMPLIANCE CHECKLIST

The following checklist is what both the internal and external compliance will require from you whenever they visit your restaurant.

1. Food handlers test certificate

This is a medical test all food handlers need to ensure they are fit to handle food. It is taken every six(6) months by all the staff in the restaurant, including managers. It must be done by a government-recognized hospital.

2. Fumigation certificate

Wherever there is food, you'd surely have insects and rodents. Therefore, it is important to fumigate the restaurant monthly. A certificate needs to be issued after each fumigation so you can show it to the compliance team when they come around.

3. Fire service certificate

All workers in a restaurant must be well trained in

using fire extinguishers in case there is a fire outbreak. Certificates of participation must be issued to the workers that attend the training. Also, the fire extinguishers must be renewed after every six months.

4. Water analysis certificate

In a restaurant, the water you use in preparing food for the public is very important. Reliable lab personnel should carry out water analysis to ensure the water in the restaurant is clean and hygienic. This exercise is done every six months.

5. Food permit certificate

This is a certificate issued by the local government of your city as evidence that you have the license to run a food business in the environment. This certificate is meant to be renewed every year.

6. Radio/TV usage certificate

This is a certificate issued by the local government for the use of sound systems in your restaurant. It is also renewed yearly.

7. LAWMA payment

This is the payment made to LAWMA for disposing of your restaurant's waste. The waste must be discarded at least four times a week.

The above certificates must be made available in your restaurant any time the compliance team visits to avoid the closure of the restaurant.

ABOUT THE AUTHOR

 Kufre Bassey has a BSc degree in Hotel and Catering Management from National Open University of Nigeria. He is also HACCP certified.

He has 18 years of work experience in the hospitality industry – in Kentucky Fried Chicken (KFC), Mr Bigg's (UAC), and Mama Cass Restaurant Limited (MCRL).

He is a passionate trainer and mentor in his field as a restaurant manager.

Kufre lives with his wife, Joyce, and their daughter in Lagos, Nigeria.